Aeroplane Friends

Written by Michelle Mohrweis

Illustrated by Sol Salinas

Collins

Chapter 1

"Paper aeroplanes are easy. Friendship is not."
I say loudly, holding up the perfect paper aeroplane.

Mum sighs. "Ash, are you sure—?

"That I don't want to play outside?" I frown, looking out of the window. "Yep."

Kiana and Lizzie are playing in the park outside. Their loud laughter dances all over the building. I could go and join them, except …

"I don't want to right now," I tell Mum. "Really. I'm having fun."

Mum sighs again.

"I promise I'm fine," I lie.

Mum stares at me like she knows. I gulp, clinging to my paper aeroplane. The paper crinkles under my fingers, getting all messed up, but that's OK. I can make a new one.

I turn to the table and grab another piece of paper.

How to make a paper aeroplane

Check that the paper isn't too thick, or it won't fly very well. Does it seem OK?

Great. Start folding!

1. Centre fold.

2. Open.

3. Pull the corners in.

4. Flatten the folds.

5. Pull the corners to the centre again.

6. Flatten so it's almost a triangle shape.

7. Fold in half.

8. Fold down one wing.

9. Flip it over.

10. Fold down the other wing.

Done. Easy peasy.

It's much easier than trying to make friends again.

I keep working on my aeroplane until Mum shakes her head and finally walks away. Then I flop onto the table.

Outside, Lizzie and Kiana laugh again, loud and happy. I bet they're sharing jokes or talking about hilarious books.

I bet it would be fun to be friends with them.

No. Nope. No.

Paper aeroplanes are easier, more reliable.

Paper aeroplanes don't pretend to be nice to me so I think I'm doing friendship 'right', but then never invite me to play with them.

Paper aeroplanes never say "maybe next time" when I ask if they want to draw comics together, but then next time never comes.

Paper aeroplanes don't avoid me just because they don't understand me.

I don't need friends. I'm fine on my own.

Still, when I pick up my finished aeroplane, I can't help writing a note in it. A letter to the universe.

I fold the aeroplane back up and carry it to the balcony.

I pull open the door, squint at the light outside, and stick out a finger to test the air. Then I pull back my arm and throw the aeroplane with all my might.

It soars!

It flips!

It glides!

Then it **CRASHES** into the building across the road, crumpling into a paper mess. Just like all my attempts at making friends.

"It's fine." I mutter, turning away. My eyes burn, but I won't cry. "I don't need friends."

Hello! To anyone who reads this:
Want to be friends?

Chapter 2

Mum says friendship is like a recipe:

1. Meet somebody new.

2. Talk about something you both find fun.

3. Become friends!

She makes it sound so easy. But Mum's friendship recipe must be missing a secret ingredient. No matter how hard I try, the recipe never works for me.

"It's fine," I mutter to myself as I colour in a panel on the comic book I'm drawing. "I have Liz."

I've been working on the comic book since the summer holidays started. It's all about a brave adventurer: Liz Flier.

Liz is autistic (like me) and she loves aeroplanes (also like me). Except, Liz doesn't make paper aeroplanes. She has her own real aeroplane that she goes on adventures in, like I'd like to do one day. Unlike me, Liz Flier never has trouble making friends.

She totally knows the secret ingredient to the friendship recipe.

I'm drawing a scene where Liz has crashed on a deserted island. She needs to find parts to fix her aeroplane.

Except, I don't know what to draw next.

"Hmm …" I bite my pencil and stare at the comic, like it can give me answers.

Nope. Still no idea.

THUD!

Then something hits the window!

I whirl around and stare. There's nothing there.
When I rush outside, I still don't see anything. I start
towards the railing, then freeze at a loud **CRUNCH**.
Is that … a paper aeroplane?

It's not one I made, so where did it come from?

Slowly I pick up the aeroplane and unfold it ...

... Inside is a letter!

I got your letter! I really, really want a friend too!

Do you like comics? What about books? Trains? Films? What school do you go to?

I've just moved here, and I am so scared to start school. Maybe we'll go to the same school? Write back soon!

P.S. Sorry for the mess. Paper aeroplanes are difficult to make!

When I peek over the edge of the balcony, there are more paper aeroplanes all over the ground. I look around until I notice something moving.

Across the road, a boy is standing on a balcony. He waves to get my attention. He looks about my age.

He cups his hands around his mouth and shouts, "Write back!"

Chapter 3

I end up back at the table, staring at the paper aeroplane letter and panicking.

What do I do? Do I reply? What should I say?

Right. Mum's friendship recipe. Step 2 is to talk about something we both find fun, which means I need to work out what the mystery boy likes to do. That means I have to write back.

I grab my best pencil and pretend I'm as brave as Liz Flier.

I don't like or hate trains, but I LOVE comics. I'm even drawing my own comic book.

I go to Cactus View. I think they call it that because of the saguaro cactus in front of the school. It's tall and really prickly.

Were there any cacti (that's the word for more than one cactus) where you lived before? Why did you move here? Do you like comics?

When I go back outside to throw the aeroplane,
the mystery boy is still sitting on his balcony.
He jumps up and waves again.

I lean a little over the balcony railing. I stick up
a finger to feel the air, then pull back my arm
and throw.

My aeroplane soars all the way across the road, up to
the other building, and onto Mystery Boy's balcony.

Ha! Perfect landing!

He jumps up and down, before grabbing my aeroplane and reading it. Then he writes on a new piece of paper and folds another aeroplane.

I watch as he throws it hard enough for it to sail across the road … then crash into the bushes below my balcony.

Oops.

Mystery Boy doesn't look upset. He laughs, then writes a new letter and tries again.

That one makes it all the way to me!

You're making a comic book? That is the coolest thing EVER! I love reading comics! Someday I want to write a comic or a story.

I'm going to Cactus View too, once the holidays are over!

Dad and Papa moved here for work. I miss my home and the trees, but seeing a cactus for the first time ever was cool. We didn't have any where I lived before. Also, our flat is bigger than our old one, so Dad says we can build a model train set in the living room. I'm so excited!

By the way, your paper aeroplanes are AMAZING.
How do you make them? Can you teach me?

Chapter 4

My new aeroplane friend and I send notes back and forth all day.

I send him instructions to make paper aeroplanes that fly straighter and catch the wind better, so he won't miss my balcony when throwing them.

He writes back the secrets for how to do
a perfect handstand. I tell him about Liz Flier.
He tells me about his favourite comics.

All day long we write letters and send them flying.

I'm having so much fun writing paper aeroplane
letters that I don't want to go inside when the sun sets.

"Ash, it's time for dinner. Come and sit down," laughs Mum as she peeks outside. "You can send more letters tomorrow."

"But Muuuum …"

"Ash. Dinner. Food. I made your favourite."

OK, that's worth stopping for. I wave goodbye to Mystery Boy, then dart inside. The kitchen smells so good, like warm rolls and melted butter.

While we eat dinner, I tell Mum all about my new paper aeroplane friend.

"… and I think your friendship recipe worked!"

"I'm so happy for you," says Mum with a smile so big that it makes me smile too. "What's your new friend's name?"

Oh.

Oh no.

I forgot to ask his name!

That night my head is too stuffed with worries for me to sleep.

What if Mystery Boy is annoyed that I forgot to ask his name? What if he doesn't want to keep writing aeroplane letters? What if I have messed everything up?

I worry and worry all night long. In the morning,
I still don't know what to do.

Do I ask for his name?

Do I tell him mine?

What if he realises that I forgot and gets angry?
What if he never wants to write to me again?

25

I worry and worry and worry until …

THUNK.

A paper aeroplane hits the door. I run to the balcony and grab it.

I gulp and open the letter.

I FORGOT TO ASK YOU YOUR NAME!
I'm so sorry!

My name is Diego Barrera-Lopez.
What's yours?

From,
Diego

27

I let out a big sigh of relief.

Diego wasn't angry. Better yet, he understands!

I quickly write back.

I'm Ash Martin.

I forgot to ask your name, too, and was scared you might be annoyed about it!

I always forget to ask about names. Mum says it's an important part of a conversation, but I get excited and forget.

– Ash

I get excited and forget too!

Even worse, sometimes I learn a person's name ... but then forget it later! It's embarrassing! Do you do that too?

From,
Diego

All the time!

That's why I decided Liz Flier (from the comics I'm drawing) will never forget a name. Liz Flier has the best memory ever.

Do you want to read my Liz Flier comic? Mum has a printer that can copy stuff too, so I can make you a copy.

– Ash

Chapter 5

I write to Diego almost every day that week. It's so much fun! We talk about *everything*.

Mum took me to the transport museum. Have you been there? It was so cool. They had an old plane hanging from the ceiling!

Also, there was a whole room all about trains. I didn't look at it much since trains are just OK, but you like them so you might like it.

It did give me ideas for Liz Flier's next adventure though.

– Ash

Excuse me? TRAINS ARE MORE THAN JUST OK! They are the best thing ever and I am going to convince you of that one day.

Now tell me more about Liz!

From,
Diego

OK, so you know how Liz was searching for the lost treasure on the island? There's going to be a secret path to an old railway track. She follows it and finds a map in a forgotten carriage!

Except I can't decide where the map should lead. What do you think?

– Ash

What if the map leads to a clue hidden in some old caves? Maybe it was made by some children who explored the caves. Only, they never finished the map or solved the clue before they left the island!

From,
Diego

That's perfect!

Maybe I really will finish my comic before the end of summer!

– Ash

I wish the holidays weren't ending. I'm so nervous about school.

I think better when I'm moving around. I can't stay still even if I want to! Papa says that's OK and that he's the same way. But sometimes teachers get annoyed by it!

From,
Diego

Don't be scared! The teachers at Cactus View are really nice.

I'm autistic and ADHD. I get overwhelmed if stuff is too loud, so last year my teacher let me wear headphones. Mum says the new teacher will, too.

Maybe there's something that can help you like that?

– Ash

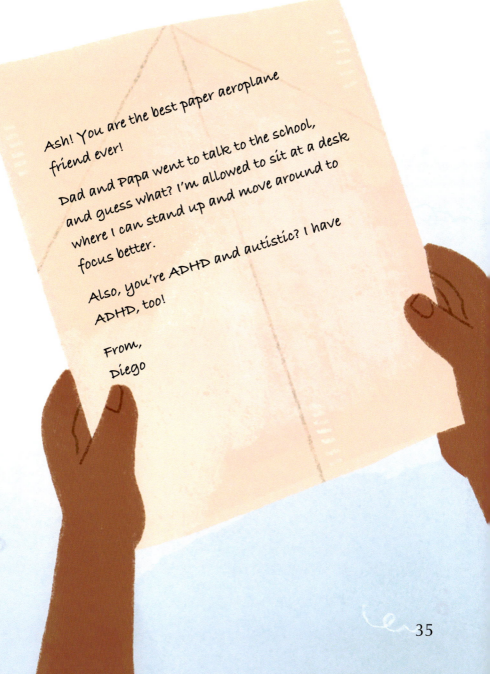

Ash! You are the best paper aeroplane friend ever!

Dad and Papa went to talk to the school, and guess what? I'm allowed to sit at a desk where I can stand up and move around to focus better.

Also, you're ADHD and autistic? I have ADHD, too!

From,
Diego

35

Chapter 6

All day, every day, Diego and I send letters back and forth. It's the best summer ever.

At least, it is until Diego sends *that* letter …

Do you want to meet properly?

Papa says I can go to the park next to your building if I'm careful crossing the road.
Let's meet there before the end of the summer holidays!

From,
Diego

I don't write Diego a letter that day. Instead, I hide inside until it's almost dinner time and Mum comes out of her office.

"Ash?" Mum peers around the corner at me. "Are you OK?"

I shake my head.

"Do you want to talk about it?" asks Mum. She sits next to me.

I shake my head again. My words are stuck inside me, all mixed up like the pile of aeroplane letters on my desk.

"Do you want to write about it?"

I shrug.

"That's OK," Mum assures me. "You don't have to."

I close my eyes and listen to the sounds of my home.

The rattling of the air conditioning. The whistle of the wind outside. The buzzing of the fridge in the kitchen. The familiar sounds help my words unglue one at a time.

"Diego wants to meet me at the park," I finally explain.

"Isn't that a good thing?" asks Mum.

"What if he doesn't like me?" I sniffle. "What if he doesn't want to be my friend after he meets me for real? The friendship recipe *never* works for me."

39

"Do you want to know a secret?" asks Mum.

I nod.

"The friendship recipe doesn't always work, and that's OK. Even I have trouble making friends sometimes. But I promise it will work this time."

"How do you know?" I ask.

"It already has." Mum points at the pile of letters on the table. "You're already friends, whether you meet at the park or not."

I stare at the pile of letters. It's a big pile. We've been writing all summer long. Would Diego really write to me that much if he didn't want to be my friend?

Mum nudges me.

"What would Liz Flier do?" she asks.

Liz Flier is the bravest person ever, like I want to be.

"OK, I'll try." I take a deep breath. Then I hop off the sofa and run to get my pencils.

When I'm finished, I throw the paper aeroplane as best I can, then wait and wait for Diego's reply.

Meet at the park this afternoon?

– Ash

See you there!

From,
Diego

"Mum! I'm going out to the park!" I announce.

"Have fun," she laughs. "Come back in time for dinner."

I run for the door, leap down the stairs, and skid across the courtyard gravel. Then I'm at the park, and—

"Ash!"

"Diego!"

"Let's go and play!"

45

Friendship Recipe

1. Meet somebody new. (Like Diego!)

2. Talk about things you both like. (I wrote letters and turned them into paper aeroplanes.)

3. Become friends. (We don't always like all the same things, but it's fun to spend time with Diego anyway. He understands me!)

46

Ideas for reading

Written by Gill Matthews
Primary Literacy Consultant

Reading objectives:
- discuss the sequence of events in books and how items of information are related
- make inferences on the basis of what is being said and done
- answer and ask questions

Spoken language objectives:
- use relevant strategies to build their vocabulary
- articulate and justify answers, arguments and opinions
- use spoken language to develop understanding through speculating, hypothesising, imagining and exploring ideas

Curriculum links: Relationships education: Caring friendships; Respectful relationships

Word count: 2597

Interest words: reliable, pretend, avoid, understand

Resources: paper

Build a context for reading

- Ask children to look at the front cover of the book and to read the title.
- Discuss what they think the book might be about.
- Read the back cover blurb. Ask what they think might happen in the story.

Understand and apply reading strategies

- Read pp2-9 aloud, using meaning, punctuation and dialogue to help you to read with appropriate expression.
- Ask children what impression they get of Ash. Ask why they think they say they don't want to play outside.
- Explore children's responses to the final sentence on p9.